Contents

Steve Parker

OXFORD

The last match

It is October 2000. England is playing football against Germany at Wembley **Stadium** in London. The stadium is packed with fans.

England's last match at the old Wembley Stadium was a **qualifying** game for the 2002 World Cup. The Final score was 1–0 to Germany.

Wembley has seen many big events but the stadium is now too old. The seats are cramped. Some seats are so far from the pitch, fans cannot see the action. There are queues for almost everything.

BUILDING WEMBLEY TIMELINE

- **2000**
- 2001
- 2002
- 2003
- 2004
- 2005
- 2006
- 2007

It's time to build a new Wembley Stadium. A bigger, better one!

A new start

Plans for the new Wembley Stadium are just beginning. The planners have to decide what the stadium will look like.

The plans for the new stadium are discussed.

The plans for the new stadium are made on computers and big sheets of paper. Every part is included, from the huge roof arch to the door handles.

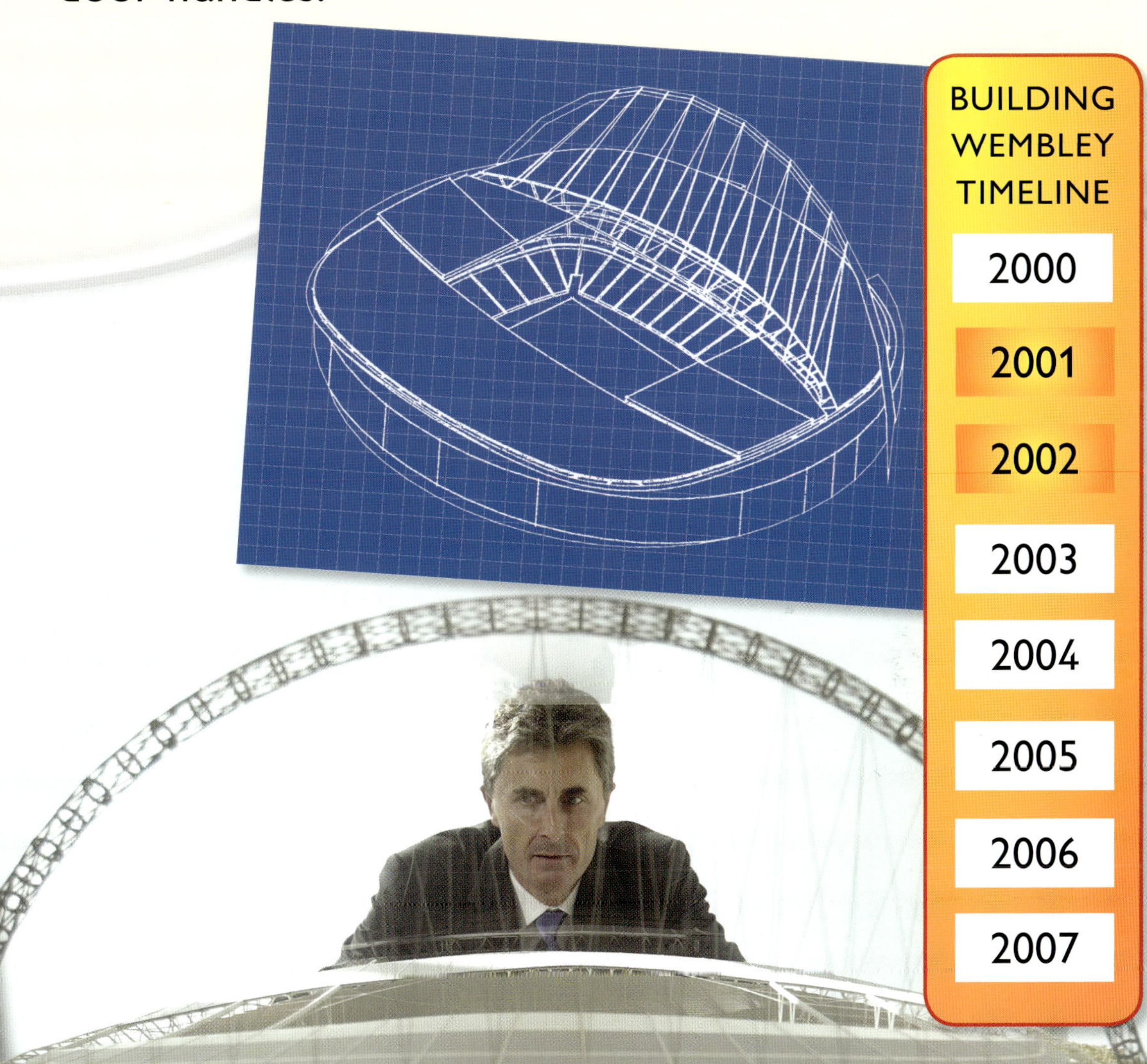

BUILDING WEMBLEY TIMELINE

- 2000
- **2001**
- **2002**
- 2003
- 2004
- 2005
- 2006
- 2007

People come to see a model of the new stadium. Everyone must agree that this is the best **design**.

Knocking it down

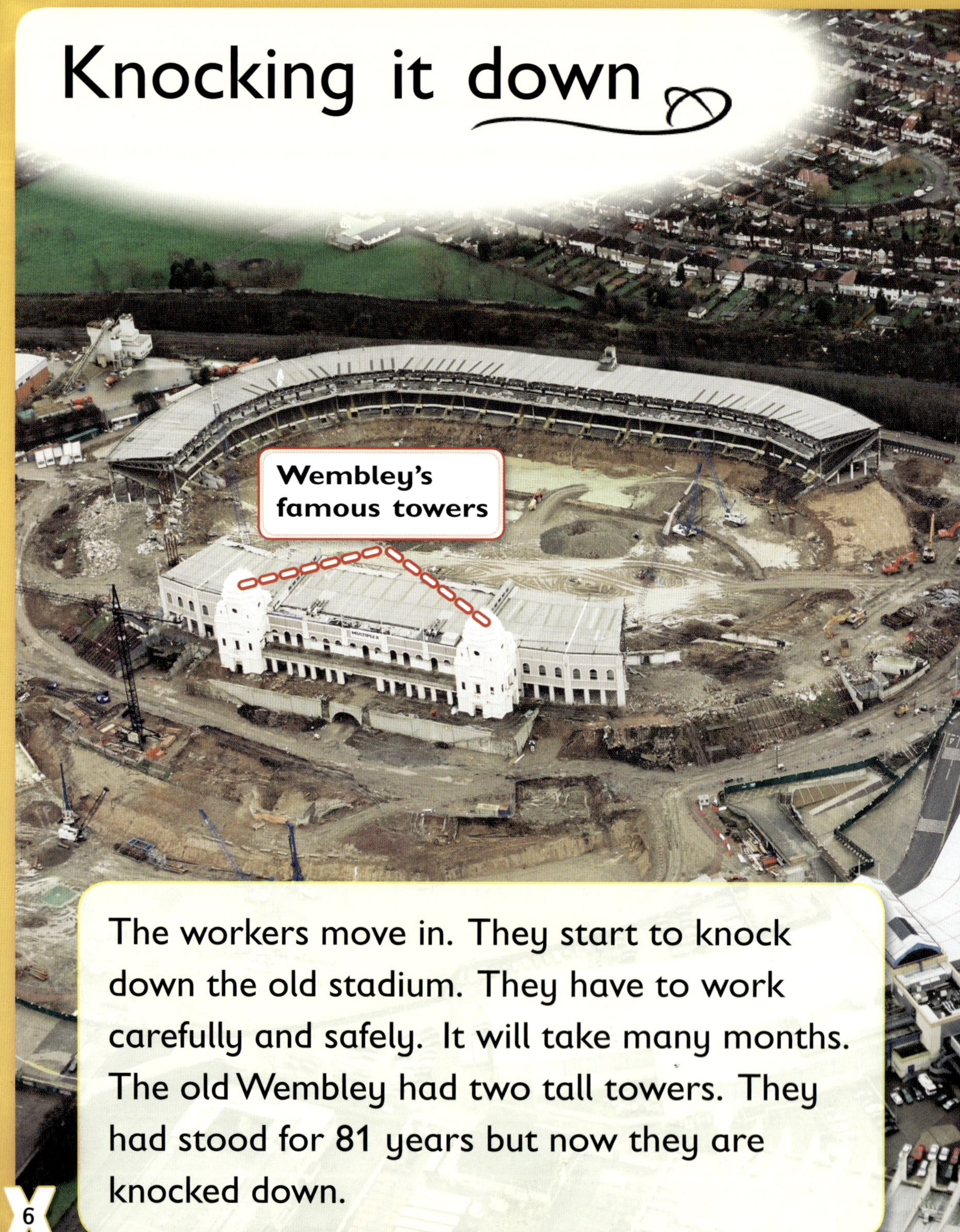

The workers move in. They start to knock down the old stadium. They have to work carefully and safely. It will take many months. The old Wembley had two tall towers. They had stood for 81 years but now they are knocked down.

Now the site is clear, work on the new stadium can begin. Posts mark where the walls, towers and pitch will go.

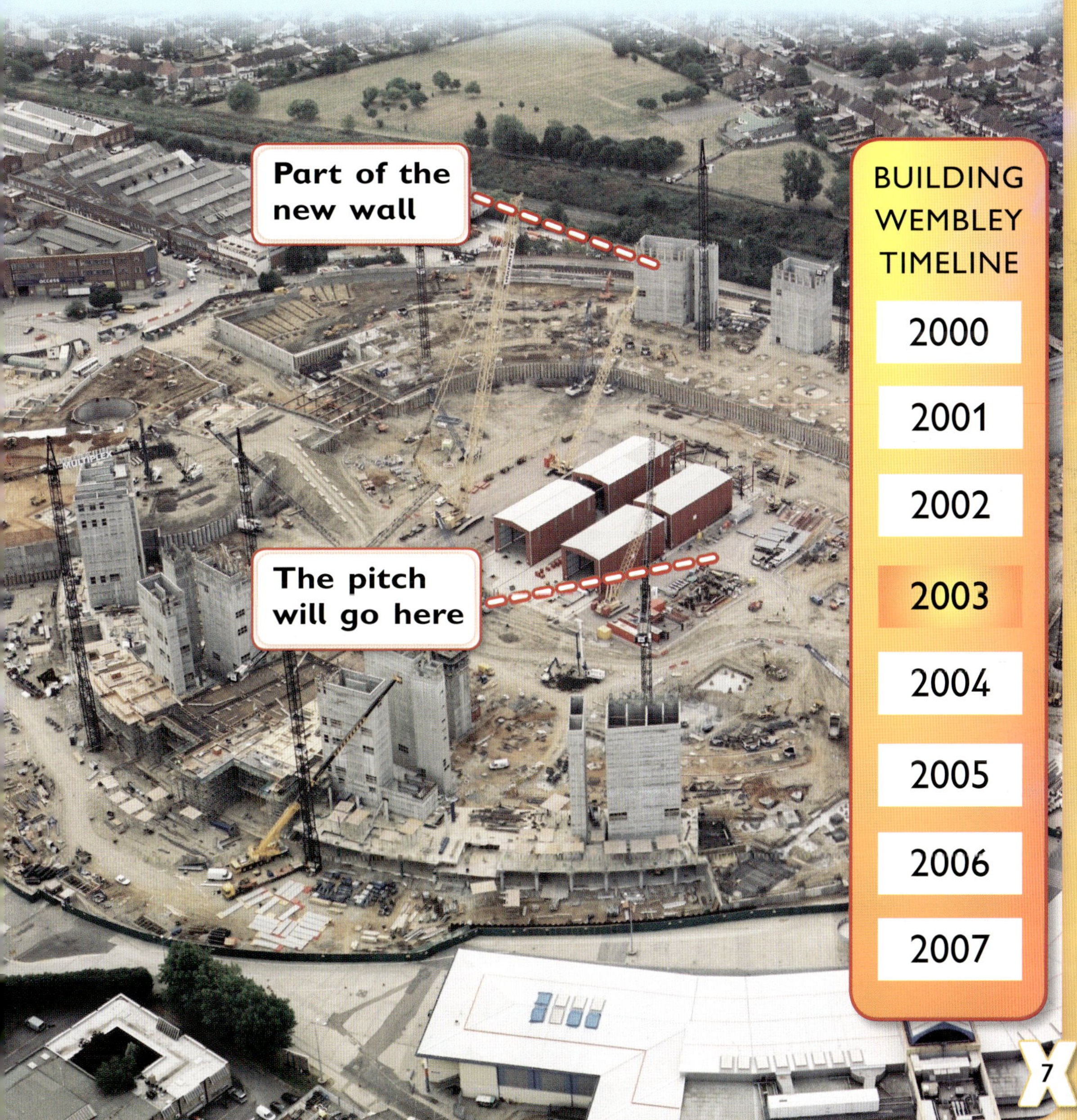

Big holes

Work on the new stadium has started but it's going down, not up! First, lots of holes must be dug.

These huge holes will be the rooms and car parks.

Diggers make long holes called trenches. These are for the electricity **cables** and water pipes.

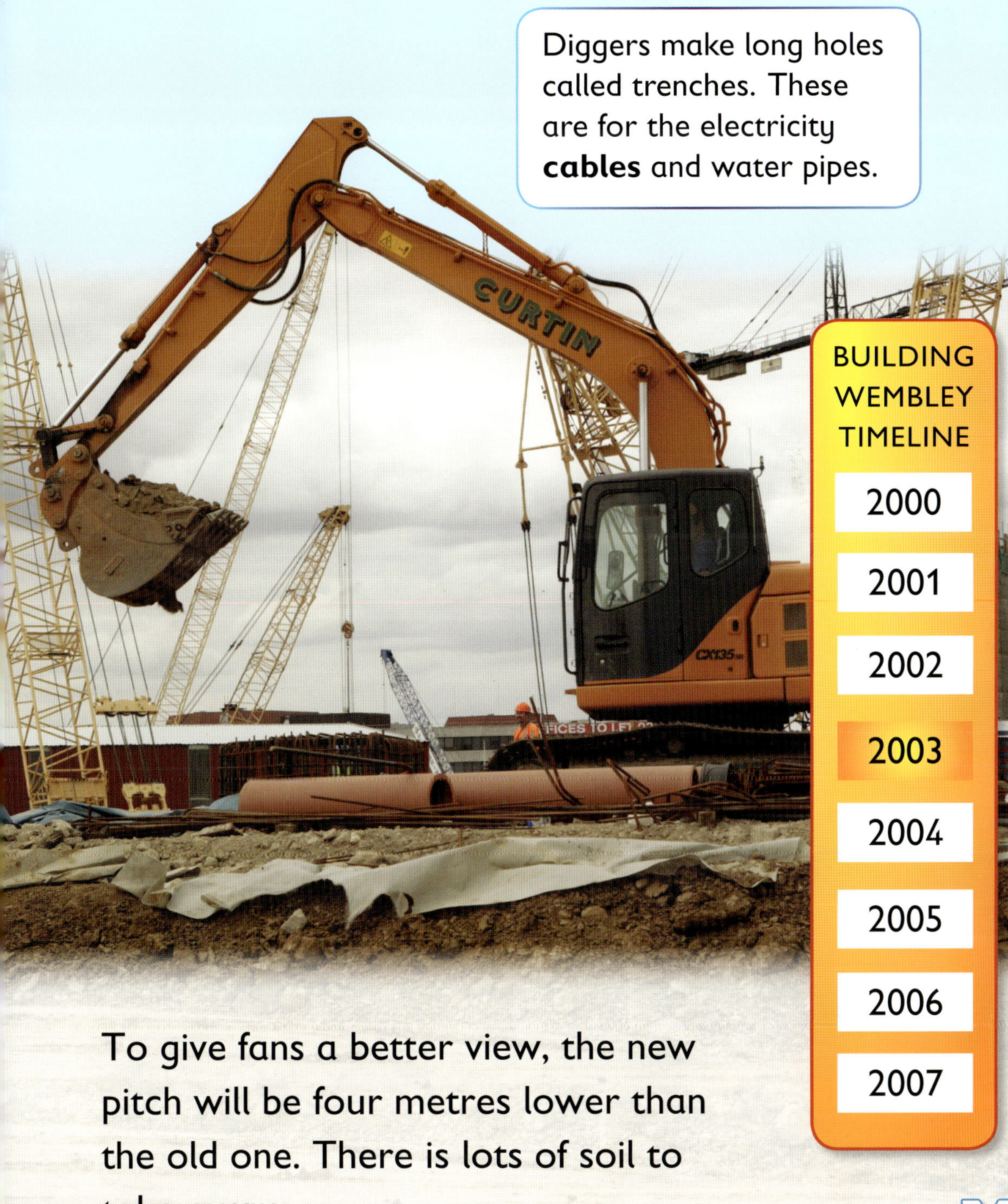

BUILDING WEMBLEY TIMELINE

2000
2001
2002
2003
2004
2005
2006
2007

To give fans a better view, the new pitch will be four metres lower than the old one. There is lots of soil to take away.

Building starts

1. Trucks start to arrive with the building materials.

2. Huge drills make holes in the ground for rods (called piles).

3. Trucks pour concrete around the piles. The concrete hardens. This will be the strong **base** for the new stadium.

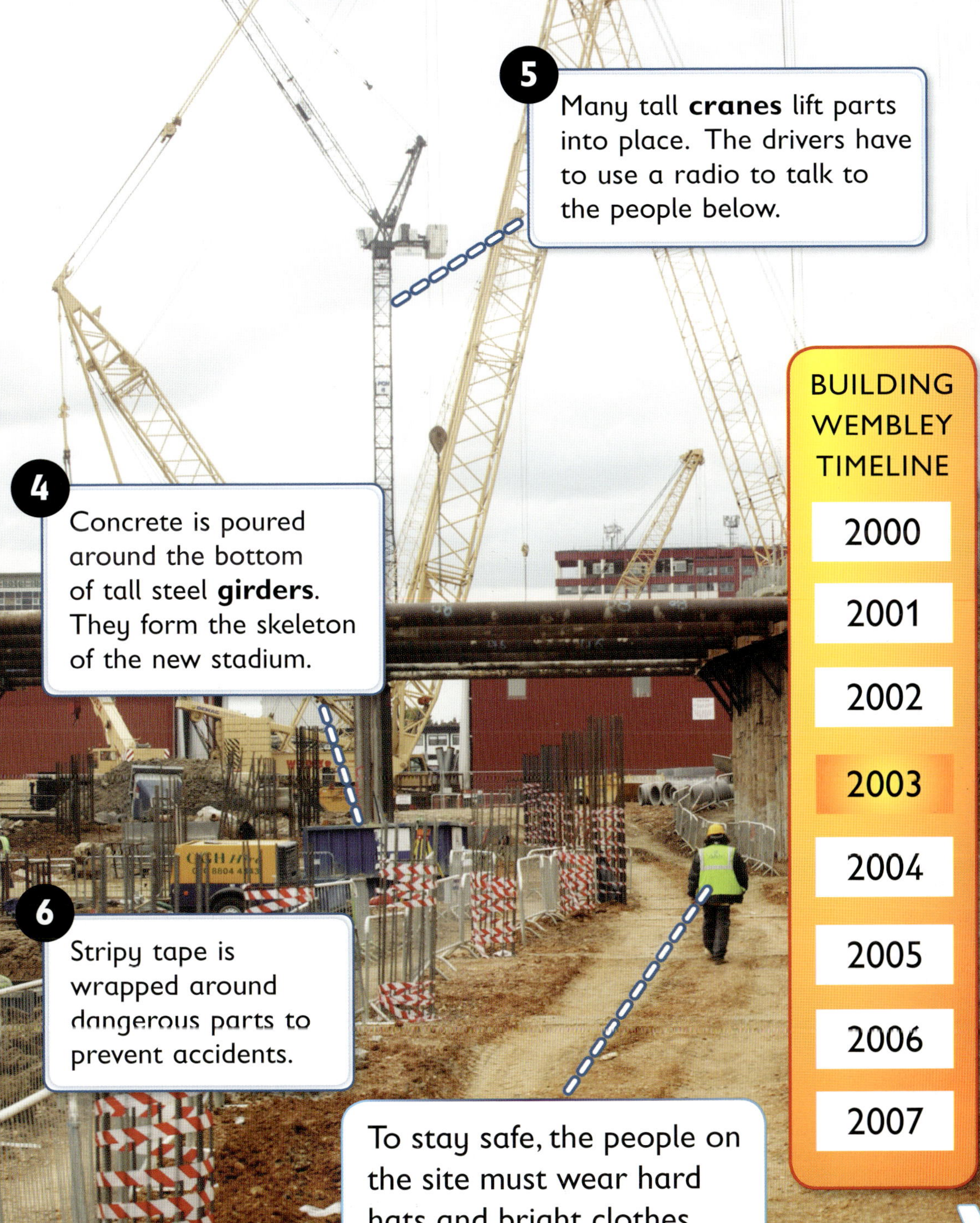
5
Many tall **cranes** lift parts into place. The drivers have to use a radio to talk to the people below.
4
Concrete is poured around the bottom of tall steel **girders**. They form the skeleton of the new stadium.
6
Stripy tape is wrapped around dangerous parts to prevent accidents.
To stay safe, the people on the site must wear hard hats and bright clothes.
BUILDING WEMBLEY TIMELINE
2000
2001
2002
2003
2004
2005
2006
2007

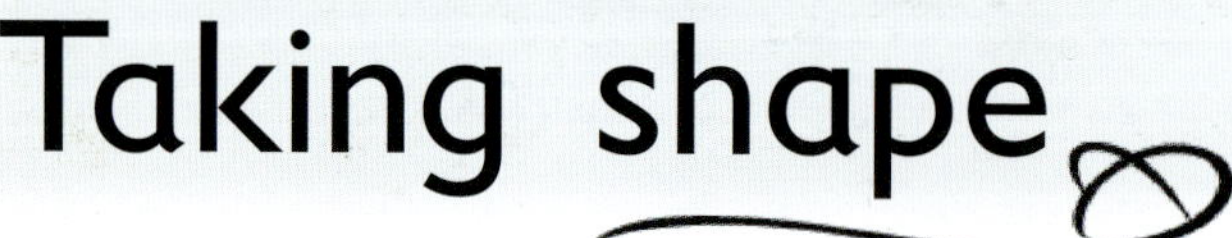

Taking shape

The stadium starts to take shape. The tall beams and strong girders will hold up the seats. The site is now very busy. There are more than 2000 workers.

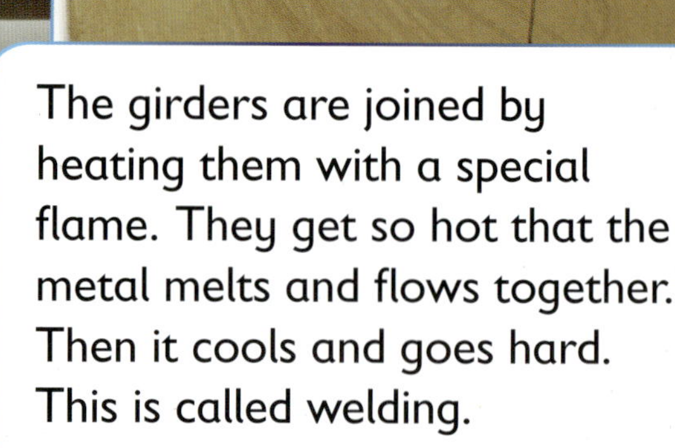

The girders are joined by heating them with a special flame. They get so hot that the metal melts and flows together. Then it cools and goes hard. This is called welding.

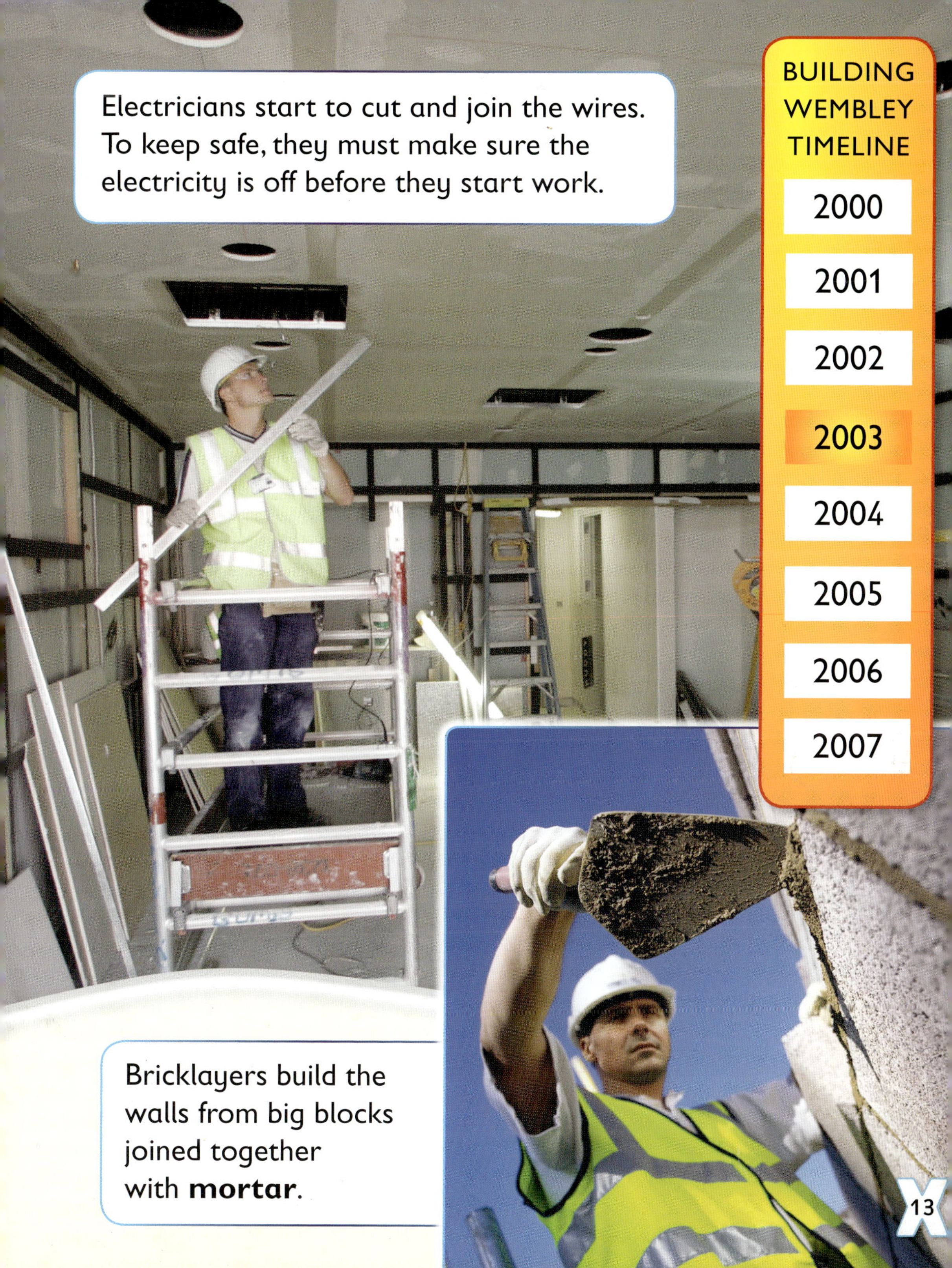

Electricians start to cut and join the wires. To keep safe, they must make sure the electricity is off before they start work.

Bricklayers build the walls from big blocks joined together with **mortar**.

The Wembley arch

The two towers have been knocked down. The new stadium will have a huge steel arch that is higher than the towers.